WHY IN THE WORLD

THE REASON GOD BECAME ONE OF US

WHY IN THE WORLD

THE REASON GOD BECAME ONE OF US

ANDY STANLEY

ZONDERVAN™

ZONDERVAN

Why in the World Participant's Guide

This title is also available as a Zondervan ebook. Visit www.zondervan.com/ebooks.
Requests for information should be addressed to:
Zondervan, *3900 Sparks Dr. SE, Grand Rapids, Michigan 49546*

ISBN 978-0-310-68225-7

First Printing June 2015 / Printed in the United States of America

CONTENTS

INTRODUCTION

Unexpected

Christians believe a lot of crazy things. One of the crazy things we believe is that God became one of us. If you grew up in the church, you heard that all the time. But have you ever stopped to consider what a strange thought it is? The Creator of the universe became a human being and walked around among other human beings.

Why in the world would he do that?

In his gospel, John says, "The Word became flesh and made his dwelling among us. We have seen his glory, the glory of the one and only Son, who came from the Father, full of grace and truth."

John was an eyewitness. After spending a lot of time with Jesus, he came to believe that Jesus was the Son of God. Then Jesus was crucified, and John assumed he must have been wrong about Jesus because no one—not even the Roman Empire—could crucify the Son of God. But three days later, John peered into an empty tomb and realized his original instinct was correct. Jesus really was the Son of God.

John wrote his gospel—wrote, "the Word became flesh"—when he was an old man, many years after Jesus had died and risen from the dead. He wrote because he had been an eyewitness to all that Jesus had done, and John knew he wouldn't live much longer. He felt compelled to pass down to future generations what he'd seen. That's because what he'd seen was so unique. It was so ... unexpected.

No one in John's time or in the centuries of Judaism that came before expected God to come down to us. No one expected God to appear as the son of a working-class carpenter from Galilee. No one expected God to allow religious leaders to challenge and disrespect him. No one expected God to let the prefect of a backwater in the Roman Empire order his execution by crucifixion. And no one—not even his closest followers—expected him to rise from the dead three days after that execution. That's not how anyone would make up the story of God.

Why would God leave the comfort and recognition of heaven to live on this ball of dirt in a time when the best of conditions barely paralleled the worst of modern-day conditions? Why would God choose to be human in a time before morphine, penicillin, or indoor plumbing?

We think we know why he died. But what compelled him to live as one of us?

That's the question you'll explore in this study. You may already know the Sunday school answer to that question—that he came to pay for our sins. The Sunday school answer is important, but it doesn't tell the whole story. There are other reasons Jesus did what he did.

I pray those reasons help you connect with God in a whole new way.

Andy Stanley

SESSION 1

To Communicate and Demonstrate

Whether or not you're a Christian, at some point in your life someone probably made a connection in your mind between God and fear. Maybe a Sunday school teacher told you God was angry at your sin. Maybe you heard someone preaching fire-and-brimstone to apathetic students in the quad at your university. Maybe you were told that if you wanted to go to heaven instead of hell, you had to pray a prayer to accept Jesus as your personal Savior.

God is mysterious. He's difficult to figure out. He's not a white-bearded old man up in heaven. He isn't a human being at all. In Isaiah 55:8–9, God says:

"For my thoughts are not your thoughts,

neither are your ways my ways,"

declares the LORD.

"As the heavens are higher than the earth,

so are my ways higher than your ways

and my thoughts than your thoughts."

It's no wonder people sometimes see God as distant and even scary. We fear what we don't understand, and we can't fully understand God.

Many people become Christians because they want to make a favorable deal with a God they assume is full of wrath and vengeance. Their decisions have little to do with love and a lot to do with fear. For a lot of people, the foundation of their faith is a feeling that God exists and that he is at least aware of them, even if he's angry or disappointed.

But Jesus didn't come so we could be certain that God knows we exist. It's much better than that. Jesus didn't claim to *have* the best explanation of God. He claimed to *be* the best explanation of God.

DISCUSSION STARTER

What, if anything, do you do to feel close to God? What is it about that habit, practice, or approach that makes you feel God's presence?

VIDEO OVERVIEW

For Session 1 of the DVD

The Gospels record an unusual conversation between Jesus and his disciples. It happened after Jesus' resurrection. His followers were excited because they assumed he was back to stay. But Jesus told them he was going to leave them. And then he said:

> "Do not let your hearts be troubled. You believe in God; believe also in me. My Father's house has many rooms; if that were not so, would I have told you that I am going there to prepare a place for you? And if I go and prepare a place for you, I will come back and take you to be with me that you also may be where I am. You know the way to the place where I am going." (John 14:1–4)

The disciples were confused. They didn't know what Jesus was talking about. More important, the idea that Jesus would leave them wasn't in alignment with the political and cultural revolution they assumed would follow Jesus' return.

> Thomas said to him, "Lord, we don't know where you are

> going, so how can we know the way?" Jesus answered, "I am the way and the truth and the life. No one comes to the Father except through me. If you really know me, you will know my Father as well. From now on, you do know him and have seen him." (John 14:5–7)

That is a bold and controversial statement. If you're going to reject Christianity, that statement is why you should reject it. If anything offends you about Christianity, it should be Jesus' claim that he is the only way to the Father. That *is* offensive. It *is* narrow.

But it was vital that Jesus made that bold, controversial, and offensive claim. He knew something about human nature: we're inclined to try to figure out God by looking in all the wrong places.

We look to our circumstances.

We constantly try to piece together events to identify God's activity in our lives. The problem is we're terrible at interpreting our circumstances. We see God where we want to see him, and ignore him in other circumstances when that interpretation doesn't fit with who we want God to be in our lives. Or we assume we know what God is up to, and then our worlds are rocked when our circumstances suddenly change.

We look to our religious traditions.

If you were raised in a church, you have some beliefs and some thoughts about God that were ingrained in you as a child. Based on your religious tradition, you have built-in assumptions about what God values, which sins most displease him, and which he doesn't get worked up about. Usually, God is more lenient with us than with outsiders. Others' sins are offensive to him, while ours are no big deal. The problem is traditions systematize, customize, overemphasize, and fossilize. *All* traditions do this.

We look within.

The other place we look to try to figure out God is within. The problem with looking within is that it'll only get you so far. Within is limited to what's within. God's bigger than whatever is within you. And here's the other thing we know: the 16-year-old version of within is different than the 30-year-old version of within, which is different than the 65-year-old version of within. Which one is God?

We look to nature.

Nature is great. Nature can teach us some things about God at the macro level. But the problem is that nature is like flying over a big city in a jet. The view is beautiful when you're in the air, but the streets can be dirty and dangerous. Nature from a distance is magnificent. Nature up close can kill you. Which represents God?

We don't have to look to our circumstances, religious traditions, within, or to nature to find out what God is like. God wants us to know him. He became one of us to communicate and demonstrate what he is like. Isn't that powerful? It means that if you move past Jesus, you're moving away from God. If you stop short of Jesus, you stop short of insights about God that would help you in your life and further your understanding of what God wants for you.

VIDEO NOTES

God showed up in a body + dwelt among us. Why?

- To communicate + demonstrate what God is ~~about~~ like + who God is
- To explain God to you (Jesus said)
- He came to take 'OVER'! Tony Evans

Homework (on pg. 19)

- Read (one) Matthew, Mark, Luke or John
- What do I learn about the Father ~~about~~ from the son

WYHseries.org

Praise
Repent
Ask
Yield

DISCUSSION QUESTIONS

1. In what ways have you seen people look in the wrong places to discover what God is like? How did it shape the ways they view God?

2. Do you tend to feel closer to God when your circumstances are good or bad? Why do you think that is the case?

3. Read John 1:14. What do you think it means that Jesus is "the Word"? What does it tell us about Jesus' connection to God?

4. During the message, Andy said, "Jesus didn't claim to *have* the best explanation of God. He claimed to *be* the best explanation of God." Respond to that statement. In what ways do you find it challenging, disturbing, or offensive?

5. Talk about some of the wrong places you've looked to find out what God is like—religious traditions, your circumstances, nature, within yourself. What limitations did you discover in these attempts to find God?

6. At the end of the message, Andy challenged you to read the four Gospels with this question in mind: What do we learna bout the Father from the Son? Which gospel will you begin with? What can this group do to help you follow through on this homework?

MOVING FORWARD

Pick one of the Gospels: Matthew, Mark, Luke, or John. Matthew has the most references to the Old Testament. Mark is the shortest. Luke is the most chronological. John is the most personal. Pick whichever one you want and begin to read it with this question in mind:

What do I learn about the Father from the Son?

CHANGING YOUR MIND

And the Word became flesh, and dwelt among us,
and we saw His glory, glory as of the only begotten
from the Father, full of grace and truth.

John 1:14 NASB

PREPARATION FOR SESSION 2

To prepare for Session 2, use these devotions during the week leading up to your small group meeting.

Day One

Read John 14:1–4. Think about the things that currently trouble your heart. How might Jesus' promises in these verses change the influence those things have over your emotions and decision making?

By taking away my anxiety + overwhelm on things to do + finish because of the move

Day Two

Read John 14:5–7. Consider the ways you look for direction from God. How does Jesus' answer in verses 6–7 differ from the kind of answer you usually want from God? Why do you think Jesus would offer himself as an answer to a question about direction?

Because its not really about 'direction' per se but about faith + trust + belief Jesus is way to Father

Day Three

Read John 14:8–14. Think about what Jesus tells you about God's character and values. Is there anything you wish you knew about God that you can't discover in Jesus? No If so, why do you think God chose not to reveal that about himself?

Day Four

Read John 14:13. How difficult is it for you to believe what Jesus says in this verse? If what Jesus says is true, what does that say about the way God views you? That I am "in"! + 'eligible' to ask for anything in Jesus' name

Day Five

Read John 9:1–34. Read this story two or three times, familiarizing yourself with its details. As you read, try to put yourself in the shoes of the blind man. Then try to experience the story as one of the Pharisees experienced it. Done

SESSION 2

Like Son, Like Father

Do you ever wonder if your suffering is your fault? Do you ever wonder if something bad in your adult life is because God is punishing you for something you did in childhood or during your college years? Most of us assume that if something bad happens, it's because we did something wrong. So we search and think and try to figure out how we can undo whatever it is we've done. We confess all sorts of stuff. We try to get on God's good side so he'll end our suffering.

That may sound silly, but most of us view suffering like that to some extent. Even Jesus' disciples thought that was how a relationship with God worked. In John 9, there's a story about one of Jesus' miracles:

> As he went along, he saw a man blind from birth. His disciples asked him, "Rabbi, who sinned, this man or his parents, that he was born blind?" (John 9:1–2)

The disciples assumed that this man's disability was the result of someone doing something to anger God—either the man or his parents. Jesus' response to the disciples' assumption is fascinating:

> "Neither this man nor his parents sinned," said Jesus, "but this happened so that the works of God might be displayed in him. As long as it is day, we must do the works of him who sent me. Night is coming, when no one can work. While I am in the world, I am the light of the world." (John 9:3–5)

This was a brand-new category for the disciples. It was a brand-new theological concept. They'd never considered that God would not simply punish with pain, but that he might have purpose in pain. They'd never considered that God might glorify himself through somebody's pain.

Last session, you were challenged to read one of the Gospels and ask, "What do I learn about the Father from the Son?" In this session, we'll dig a little deeper into this story of Jesus' miraculous healing of a blind man and discover three things we can learn about God from Jesus' behavior.

DISCUSSION STARTER

Talk about a time when you overcame adversity, large or small. What did you learn from that experience?

VIDEO OVERVIEW

For Session 2 of the DVD

When we see people who trust God through pain, it does something for our faith. It makes us think, *"I don't need that kind of grace right now, but I'm glad to know it exists. When my time comes, I'll know I can tap into it."* Jesus introduced this idea of trusting God in the midst of pain when he healed the man who had been blind from birth. The disciples were thinking in terms of sin and retribution. But Jesus shifted the conversation to the topics of God's glory and power. The disciples had no clue that God might have a purpose in the blind man's pain. They had never considered that God might want to display his power in our pain. They learned something about the Father from the Son.

John's gospel tells us that Jesus healed the man. His neighbors were blown away because they'd known the man his whole life and he'd always been blind. He was born that way. Now, he could see. So, they took action:

> They brought to the Pharisees the man who had been blind. Now the day on which Jesus had made the mud and opened the man's eyes was a Sabbath. Therefore the Pharisees also asked him how he had received his sight. "He put mud on my eyes," the man replied, "and I washed, and now I see." Some of the Pharisees said, "This man is not from God, for he does not keep the Sabbath." (John 9:13–16)

Jesus healed a blind man—performed a miracle—but the religious leaders were more concerned about whether performing a healing constituted breaking the Sabbath law. When they pressed the formerly blind man on the issue of whether Jesus was a sinner, here's what the man said:

> He replied, "Whether he is a sinner or not, I don't know. One thing I do know. I was blind but now I see!" (John 9:25)

The Pharisees were concerned about religion, but Jesus showed up to make it extraordinarily clear that God's mercy flows over and past any theological system. In fact, Jesus made it clear that mercy should inform our theology. That means that when theology becomes an obstacle to mercy, change your theology.

When your view of God leads you to believe someone is outside of God's mercy and grace, there's something wrong with your view of

God. We could never understand how broad and deep God's mercy is if it weren't for Jesus showing up and correcting our thinking.

Here are three things we can learn about the Father from the Son's interaction with the man who was born blind:

God sometimes chooses to display his power through our pain.

"Neither this man nor his parents sinned, but this happened so that the works of God might be displayed in him," Jesus told his disciples about the blind man. On the one hand that's a scary thought: God is sometimes more concerned with his own glory than with our pain. On the other hand, that thought is liberating. It's a reminder that God isn't out to punish us for our wrongdoing. He's on our side. And his grace and mercy are always available to us, even when we're suffering.

God extends mercy in spite of bad theology.

Take note of the healed man's response when the Pharisees asked him if Jesus was a sinner for healing him on the Sabbath. "Whether he is a sinner or not, I don't know," the man said. Jesus' decision to heal the man wasn't contingent on the man's grasp of theology. God's love and mercy is abundant. We don't have to worry that he'll withhold it from us if we're wrong, unsure, or confused about some things.

God takes personal interest in individuals.

Do you ever wonder if God knows your name? It's a common anxiety people have about God. One of the most powerful things about the ministry of Jesus is that he chose to heal *one person at a time*. In the Gospels, when Jesus heals someone, it's not an abstract theological event. It's Jesus interacting with a person ... an individual. Jesus didn't heal a crowd of blind people. He healed a blind man. One man. He didn't have to go person-to-person, but he did. Why? Because he taught us something about the Father. God cares about us individually.

These three takeaways from the story of Jesus healing a blind man can't be found in our circumstances, good or bad. They can't be discovered through religious tradition. They can't be found within ourselves or out in nature. These are things about the Father that we can only learn from the Son.

VIDEO NOTES

Sometimes God will display his power through our pain

God extends mercy beyond theology

Mercy should inform theology

God takes personal interest in every individual

DISCUSSION QUESTIONS

1. Last week, Andy asked you to read one of the Gospels with this question in mind: *"What do I learn about the Father from the Son?"* What is one insight you gained about God as you read?

2. Have you ever seen someone demonstrate great faith despite great suffering? How did that affect your faith in God?

3. Do you ever wonder if your suffering is your fault? If so, how has that shaped your view of God?

4. During the message, Andy said, *"God sometimes chooses to display his power through our pain."* Respond to that statement. How does it bother you? In what ways is it comforting?

5. During the message, Andy used an example of the Pharisees allowing their theology to become an obstacle to mercy for a man cured of blindness. In what ways have you seen theology—your own or someone else's—act as an obstacle to mercy?

6. Do you find it difficult to believe that God takes an interest in you individually? Why or why not? What is one thing you can do this week to remind yourself that God *is* interested in you individually?

MOVING FORWARD

Once upon a time, God was one of us. One of the reasons Jesus came to be one of us and to live among us was to clarify for us what our heavenly Father is like. The closer you get to Jesus, the closer you get to understanding God. If you stop short of Jesus, you stop short of understanding God. If you move past Jesus, you're moving away from the Father.

If you didn't start reading one of the Gospels last week, it's not too late. Pick Matthew, Mark, Luke, or John, and just begin to read with this question in mind:

What do I learn about the Father from the Son?

CHANGING YOUR MIND

He replied, "Whether he is a sinner or not, I don't know.
One thing I do know. I was blind but now I see!"
John 9:25

PREPARATION FOR SESSION 3

To prepare for Session 3, use these devotions during the week leading up to your small group meeting.

Day One

Read Luke 7:36–39. Think about the contrast between what Jesus is focused on and what the Pharisee is focused on.

Jesus focused on the magnitude of her giving; Pharisee focused only on her sinner reputation

Day Two

Read Luke 7:39–43. The Pharisee is full of doubt about who Jesus is. With that in mind, consider the approach that Jesus takes in confronting him. What is Jesus' tone? Is he harsh or gentle? Why do you think Jesus took the approach he did? Jesus' tone was gentle + his approach was illustrative

Day Three

Read Luke 7:44–50. Focus on how Jesus responds to the woman. Consider how this might reflect his relationship with you.

Always the Forgiver for me when I repent + love

Day Four

Read Romans 5:1–5. As you read, think and pray about the connection between personal suffering, faith, and peace with God through Jesus.

Day Five

Read Romans 5:6–11. Pray that God would reveal any areas in your life where you mistakenly see yourself as an "enemy of God." Ask for his help in taking to heart the truth that Jesus loved you enough to die for you.

SESSION 3
Classless

Have you ever been picked on for something you had no control over? Most of us have. You may have faced discrimination because you're part of a group that gets picked on. Maybe something is different about you, and that drew attention from people who were cruel. Maybe you were picked on in high school because that's just what happens in high school. Whatever the specifics, if you've been discriminated against—even if it was over something small and meaningless—it was dehumanizing.

Being discriminated against throws you off balance. Even years later when no one picks on you anymore, you can't completely shake from your mind whatever it was that made you a target. You assume everyone knows but is just pretending not to notice. That's because you've internalized that pain and rejection. So, you go in one of two ways:

1. You power up.

   You make your personality bigger and bolder in order to compensate for feeling small. Maybe you develop an attitude, a chip on your shoulder.

2. You disappear.

   You try to become invisible because you're self-conscious. Maybe if no one notices you, no one will victimize you.

The good news is that one of the reasons God came into the world, one of the reasons he became one of us, was to elevate the status of *everyone*. He wanted to show the world that he valued all people—not just a select few. And if God values someone, he or she has intrinsic value that cannot be taken away by another person.

During his earthly ministry, Jesus introduced this idea that all people are valuable. That idea shook the foundation of human culture. It changed the world. If you take it to heart, it can change you too.

DISCUSSION STARTER

Think about the people you hung out with in high school. How did your association with that group benefit you? How did it influence the way you treated others?

VIDEO OVERVIEW

For Session 3 of the DVD

The authors of the United States Declaration of Independence declared it "self-evident" that all people were created equal. But self-evident is only self-evident to those who understand that there's a relationship between the Creator and the creature. Treating others as equals doesn't come naturally.

Human beings naturally gravitate toward others who are like them. We gather into groups and then treat outsiders differently than insiders. Discrimination, prejudice, and power plays are natural. We may know in our minds that others have equal value in God's eyes, but that truth doesn't easily penetrate our hearts. It doesn't feel natural for us to treat those who are different from us as though they really are valuable as individuals.

When Jesus came into this world, people were considered commodities. People were owned. There was no sense that God would hold people accountable for how they treated the people around them. Slaves had no status. The poor had no status. Women and children had no status. They were all expendable. If you were among the elite classes, you had rights. If you weren't in that group, you had little or no rights.

Jesus stepped into that world and challenged the culture's assumptions in three ways.

Through his teaching

Jesus told his followers to live differently than everyone around them. He said to them:

> "A new command I give you: Love one another. As I have loved you, so you must love one another. By this everyone will know that you are my disciples, if you love one another." (John 13:34–35)

What does it look like to reflect God's love of *all* people so radically that the world takes notice? Jesus paints a picture of God's love in the introduction to his Sermon on the Mount with a series of statements called the Beatitudes:

> "Blessed are the poor in spirit,
>   for theirs is the kingdom of heaven.
> Blessed are those who mourn,

for they will be comforted.

Blessed are the meek,

for they will inherit the earth.

Blessed are those who hunger and thirst for righteousness,

for they will be filled.

Blessed are the merciful,

for they will be shown mercy.

Blessed are the pure in heart,

for they will see God.

Blessed are the peacemakers,

for they will be called children of God.

Blessed are those who are persecuted because of righteousness,

for theirs is the kingdom of heaven.

(Matthew 6:3–10)

The idea that those who are poor in spirit, mourning, meek, persecuted, hungry for righteousness, merciful, pure in heart, and peaceful are blessed is counterintuitive. Even today, it seems a little out of step with reality. In Jesus' time, it was revolutionary. No one said things like that. No one *thought* things like that.

Jesus put the world on notice: human culture may say "might makes right," but God has a different view of things.

Through his interactions

Jesus elevated the dignity of people through his interactions with individuals. Throughout his ministry, Jesus paused and raised and gave dignity to individuals. Individuals who had no dignity. In the story of Zacchaeus, for example, Jesus goes out of his way to engage with a wealthy chief tax collector who was hated by everyone because of his collaboration with the Roman Empire.

Surrounded by a crowd that wanted to hear him speak, Jesus put everything on hold so he could connect with Zacchaeus one-on-one.

> When Jesus reached the spot, he looked up and said to him, "Zacchaeus, come down immediately. I must stay at your house today." So he came down at once and welcomed him gladly. All the people saw this and began to mutter, "He has gone to be the guest of a sinner." But Zacchaeus stood up and said to the Lord, "Look, Lord! Here and now I give half of my possessions to the poor, and if I have cheated anybody out of anything, I will pay back four times the amount." Jesus said to him, "Today salvation has come to this house, because this man, too, is a son of Abraham. For the Son of Man came to seek and to save the lost." (Luke 19:5–10)

The people in the crowd couldn't believe that Jesus had chosen to hang out with Zacchaeus. But Jesus showed them that chief tax collectors, no matter how hated by their neighbors, were valued and loved by God.

Through his death

Jesus elevated the dignity of the individual to the greatest degree through his death. If you're a Christian and you really believe that God sent his Son into the world to die for our sins, then the fact that God would view equally every single individual who ever lived—including the person you dislike the most—should change the way you view and treat *every* person.

At the cross, everybody's dignity was raised to a level we don't deserve. At the foot of the cross, we are all laid low, and we are all made equal in the sight of God.

Approximately twenty years after Jesus' resurrection, the apostle Paul said it this way:

> Very rarely will anyone die for a righteous person, though for a good person someone might possibly dare to die. But God demonstrates his own love for us in this: While we were still sinners, Christ died for us. (Romans 5:7–8)

Because he is God, Jesus was able to live without adjectives and labels. There were no "good" people and "bad" people. There were no "righteous" and "unrighteous" people. There were no "in-people" and "out-people." He didn't even make a clear distinction between Jews that were in and Gentiles that were out.

For Jesus, there were only people.

Jesus wasn't naive. He knew the hearts of all men and women. And apparently, Jesus saw that there wasn't that much difference in people's hearts. We all need God's love, grace, and mercy.

VIDEO NOTES

Opt for natural over self-evident

DISCUSSION QUESTIONS

1. In what ways do adults label people? How does this impulse to attach labels to other human beings shape our culture?

2. What labels, good or bad, do you carry? How do they shape how you see yourself?

3. During the message, Andy said, *"The Christian community should be the most nondiscriminatory, it-doesn't-matter-to-us-who-you-are group of people on the planet."* What are some of the obstacles to the church living up to that calling? What is the cost of not living up to that calling?

4. Read Romans 5:7–8. How does this passage change the way you view your value as a human being? How does it challenge the way you view others?

5. What person or group of people do you power up around, look down on, treat as less than, or maintain a bad attitude toward? What causes you to respond to that person or group the way you do?

6. What is one thing you can do this week to begin to treat that person or group with dignity? How can this group support you?

MOVING FORWARD

In the Gospels, whenever somebody tried to take the words of God and twist them in order to alienate or hurt people, Jesus was quick to remind them that didn't reflect God's heart. At the foot of the cross, we lose our right to discriminate against anybody for any reason. The Christian community should be the most nondiscriminatory group of people in the world.

As you continue to read the Gospels, look for places in the life of Jesus where he elevated the dignity of the individual. They're everywhere. Look at how he interacts with outcasts, shepherds, working-class people, women, children, and people who are known sinners. Look at the way Jesus went out of his way to elevate the dignity of the individual, because that's one of the reasons God came into this world and dwelt among us.

CHANGING YOUR MIND

Very rarely will anyone die for a righteous person, though for a good person someone might possibly dare to die. But God demonstrates his own love for us in this: While we were still sinners, Christ died for us.

Romans 5:7–8

PREPARATION FOR SESSION 4

To prepare for Session 4, use these devotions during the week leading up to your small group meeting.

Day One

Read John 1:14. In light of all you've read, watched, and discussed during this study, is there anything you see in this verse that you didn't see before? —

Day Two

Read Mark 2:23–27. Read the passage two or three times. Based on the context, consider what it means that "the Sabbath was made for man." What implications might this have for your own life?

Not sure

Day Three

Read Isaiah 1:11, 13. As you read, pay attention to the emotion behind God's words. Why might he be passionate about this subject?

Due to His feelings about
their fallen behavior

Day Four

Read Isaiah 1:15. What does this tell you about God's desire for justice? He rights wrongs

Day Five

Read Isaiah 1:17. Think about how this verse relates to what you learned in Session 3 about the value God places on people. What are some ways you can "seek justice" in your daily life?

To increase my awareness in my behavior measured by the fruits of the Spirit

- love
- joy
- peace
- forebearance
- kindness
- goodness
- faithfulness
- gentleness
- self-control

SESSION 4

Putting Religion in Its Place

Jesus came into the world to put religion in its place.

Religion plays an important role in our culture. Not just Christianity, but all religion plays an important role because we all have questions for which religion provides context:

What happens when we die?

Will I ever see my mother again?

How big is heaven?

Does life have meaning or is it just a random series of events?

We all need rules to live by. Religion gives us principles and laws. We have ethical and moral questions. Religion provides us with ethical and moral boundaries. Religion offers some certainty in an uncertain world. It provides a framework for viewing the world around us.

It helps us to find meaning and purpose.

Religious systems are important. But when religion takes first place, it flexes its muscles at the expense of mercy. Child sacrifice, honor killings, and holy wars have all resulted from religion. The religious people were the ones who shouted, "Crucify him! Crucify him!" about Jesus.

Child sacrifice and honor killings may seem extreme—and far removed from our cultural norms and daily experiences—but an unhealthy devotion to a religious system can cause us to treat those who are different from us a little colder. It can cause us to view people who don't see the world the way we do as "less than." Religion can be an excuse to separate from people who make us uncomfortable or even abuse those we think aren't worthy of our best.

This week, we'll explore how Jesus came to challenge our assumptions about the importance of religion as well as our assumptions about what God thinks of people we don't like.

DISCUSSION STARTER

Do you tend to follow rules to the letter, bend them when it suits you, or outright break them? In what ways do you think that tendency has influenced the way you view God?

VIDEO OVERVIEW

For Session 4 of the DVD

When religion is treated as a rigid absolute, it tends to collapse under the weight of the real world. You hear someone preach a sermon about how to have a great family life. The speaker gives you a series of steps to follow, but when you get home, those steps aren't as simple or effective as they sounded on that Sunday morning you heard the sermon. That's because religious speakers and teachers often try to systematize everything. They simplify. They reduce. That's great in a sermon, but life is usually a lot messier. And God is a lot less predictable.

The other problem with religion is that when people put it in first place, they become self-righteous, hypocritical, and angry. There's a connection between self-righteousness and anger because self-righteous people secretly wish they could commit the sins they publicly denounce. This self-righteousness, hypocrisy, and anger give a lot of people the wrong idea about God and drive them out of the church. It's tragic.

But here's the interesting thing. When you read the Gospels, you find that battle against the kind of religious devotion that breeds self-righteousness, hypocrisy, and anger. Jesus and the religious leaders of his day believed the law of Moses was important. Jesus and the religious leaders of his day also believed that people were important. What they argued over was how to prioritize the law and people.

Jesus consistently prioritized people over his own religion. That's a shocking idea because Jesus is the Son of God. But he *always* prioritized people over his own religion, customs, and traditions. The Pharisees couldn't understand what Jesus was up to. From their perspective, it didn't add up that he claimed to be from God yet often appeared to compromise—or sometimes even *break*—the law. Jesus would say that no one should ever change the law of Moses, and then he would seem to disregard the law for the sake of some poor soul or someone in need. It was confusing and even offensive to the Pharisees.

One day, Jesus clarified his view of the relationship between the law and people. The story is found in Mark's gospel:

> One Sabbath Jesus was going through the grainfields, and as his disciples walked along, they began to pick some heads of grain. The Pharisees said to him, "Look, why are they doing what is unlawful on the Sabbath?" (Mark 2:23–24)

The law said you're not supposed harvest on the Sabbath. The Pharisees were trying to catch Jesus and his disciples in a technicality. The disciples were picking grain, but they weren't really harvesting. They were having a snack. Jesus responds by challenging the Pharisees' application of religion. He brings up a story from the Old Testament:

> He answered, "Have you never read what David did when he and his companions were hungry and in need? In the days of Abiathar the high priest, he entered the house of God and ate the consecrated bread, which is lawful only for priests to eat. And he also gave some to his companions." (Mark 2:25–26)

David is one of the spiritual giants of Judaism. To the Pharisees, he was untouchable. Yet Jesus pitted their rigid religious interpretations against David. He followed up that challenge with a statement that is clarifying, disturbing, and enormously important. It's a statement that makes Christianity messy and wonderful. It's a statement that may even go to the heart of what you most struggle with in terms of your relationship with the church.

> Then he said to them, "The Sabbath was made for man, not man for the Sabbath. So the Son of Man is Lord even of the Sabbath." (Mark 2:27–28)

God didn't create laws and then create human beings to keep those laws. That's backwards. The laws are important. But God created people, then created the laws so those people could better know him and what he values. Great parents decide that their children are more important than the laws the parents set. And God is a perfect heavenly Father. He created the law for people—for his children.

Sometimes great parents break the rules because their kids are more important to them than the rules they made. Sometimes they break the rules and their kids are happy. Sometimes they break the rules and their kids are angry. But they break the rules because their kids are the top priority.

That's what your heavenly Father does. It makes religious people nervous. But Jesus came to put religion in its place. It's not first place; it's second place. He never allowed theology to get in the way of ministry. He never leveraged theology in order to mistreat a person. He never leveraged theology in order to avoid helping someone.

That doesn't mean Jesus' theology was wrong or weak. He was God dwelling among us. His theology was perfect. But Jesus' conscience was formed by compassion, not consistency, because love demands inconsistency. The moment we put religion ahead of people, we move backwards, away from Jesus. Jesus was so inconsistent that instead of letting our sin separate us from our heavenly Father, he *became* our sin, allowed himself to die on a cross, and then rose from the dead in order to conquer death on our behalf. He didn't do that because that's what theology demanded. He did it because that's what love demanded.

Jesus didn't die for precepts and principles. Jesus died for people.

Jesus didn't die for the law. Jesus died for the lawless.

Jesus didn't die for a set of rules. Jesus died for rule-breakers.

Jesus didn't even die for sin. Jesus died for sinners.

Jesus didn't die for a view. Jesus died for a *you.*

You are more important to me than my view

Don't allow a view to supercede you

Jesus didn't die for the law -- he died for the lawbreakers

not for sin, but for sinners

Theology vs Ministry

VIDEO NOTES

Jesus came to:

- Demonstrate God
- To elevate the dignity of individual
- To put religion in its place

★ when religion takes 1st place it begins to flex its muscle at the expense of mercy

Religion collapses under weight of real world

Real life

Unsystematic

random

messy

Inconsistent

Leaders = self-righteous

Followers = hypocrites

Jesus consistently prioritized PEOPLE over religion, customs + traditions

① Love God. ② Love Your Neighbor

DISCUSSION QUESTIONS

1. What are some reasons people find rules comfortable and comforting?

2. Are there things about religion that you find constraining or stifling? If so, what are those things?

3. Read Isaiah 1:13, 17. How do these verses challenge most people's views of God? What do they tell us about what he values?

4. During the message, Andy said, *"Jesus consistently prioritized people over his own religion, customs, and traditions."* Respond to that statement. In what ways does it challenge your assumptions about Jesus?

5. Is it difficult for you to believe that God values you above his own rules? Why or why not?

6. What is one thing you can do this week to prioritize loving God and loving other people over your religion, customs, and traditions? What can this group do to support you?

MOVING FORWARD

Do you know what's most important to God? It's not his law. It's you. Why in the world did Jesus come as one of us? Why in the world did God show up as a human being on a planet full of strife, suffering, and injustice? One of the reasons was that he wanted to put religion—all religion—in its place. And religion's place is right behind you.

CHANGING YOUR MIND

Jesus replied: "'Love the Lord your God with all your heart and with all your soul and with all your mind.' This is the first and greatest commandment. And the second is like it: 'Love your neighbor as yourself.' All the Law and the Prophets hang on these two commandments."

Matthew 22:37–40

LEADER'S GUIDE

LEADER'S GUIDE

This Leader's Guide contains helpful tips for using these *Why in the World* materials with your group.

Leading the Discussion

You probably have a mental picture of what it will look like to lead—what you'll say and how group members will respond. Before you get too far into planning, there are some things you should know about leading a small group discussion.

Cultivate Discussion

It's easy to assume that a group meeting lives or dies on the quality of your ideas. That's not true. It's the ideas of everyone in the group make a small group meeting successful. Your role is to create an environment where people feel safe to share their thoughts. That's how relationships will grow and thrive among your group members.

Here's a basic truth about spiritual growth within the context of community: the study materials aren't as important as the relationships through which those materials take practical shape in the lives of the group members. The more meaningful the relationships, the more meaningful the study. The best materials in the world won't change lives in a sterile environment.

Point to the Material

A good host or hostess creates an environment where people can connect relationally. He or she knows when to help guests connect and when to stay out of the way when those connections are happening organically. As a small group leader, sometimes you'll simply read a discussion question and invite everyone to respond. The conversation will take care of itself. At other times, you may need to encourage group members to share their ideas. Remember, some of the best insights will come from the people in your group. Go with the flow, but be ready to nudge the conversation in the right direction when necessary.

Depart from the Material

We've carefully designed this study for your small group. We've written the materials and designed the questions to elicit the kinds of conversations we think will be most helpful to your group members. That doesn't mean you should stick rigidly to the materials. Knowing when to depart from them is more art than science, but no one knows more about your group than you do.

The stories, questions, and exercises are here to provide a framework for exploration. But different groups have different chemistries and different motivations. Sometimes the best way to start a small group discussion is to ask, "Does anyone have a personal insight you'd like to share from this week's material?" Then sit back and listen.

Stay on Track

This is the flip side to the previous point. There's an art to facilitating an engaging conversation. While you want to leave space for group members to think through the discussion, you also need to keep your objectives in mind. Make sure the discussion is contributing to the bottom line for the week. Don't let the discussion veer off into tangents. Interject politely in order to refocus the group.

Pray

This is the most important thing you can do as a leader. The best leaders get out of God's way and let him communicate through them. Remember: books don't teach God's Word; neither do sermons or discussion groups. God speaks into the hearts of men and women. Prayer is a vital part of communicating with him.

Pray for your group members. Pray for your own leadership. Pray that God is not only present at your group meetings, but is directing them.

Session 1: Notes for Leading

Big Idea

Jesus lived and taught in order to reveal the truth about the Father.

To find and understand God, look to Jesus.

To Prepare to Lead the First Session

- Read John 14.
- Pray that you and your group members begin the study with hearts and minds open to what God wants to show you.

Discussion Starter

The Discussion Starter is designed as an icebreaker. Some of the questions may feel a little random, but they're intended to help your group members warm up by talking about a common experience or tension. They're usually related in some way to the session's topic but are intended to get your group members talking about their personal experiences without delving into theology or doctrine.

The Session 1 Discussion Starter is meant to get group members talking about the private disciplines they use—reading the Bible, praying, fasting—to connect with God. Thinking about how we connect with God can get us to think about the assumptions we make about God.

Discussion Questions

1. **In what ways have you seen people look in the wrong places to discover what God is like? How did it shape the ways they view God?**

   The first question is intended to get your group thinking in more concrete ways about the wrong places we look to discover God. It is focused outwardly at the behavior of other people in order to allow group members to ease into the conversation.

2. **Do you tend to feel closer to God when your circumstances are good or bad? Why do you think that is the case?**

   Interpreting God's character or actions through our circumstances is something almost all of us do. This question encourages your group to explore that idea—including its shortcomings—on their own. As your group members talk about their experiences, it will become clearer that some people feel more connected to God when their circumstances are good, while others feel more connected when challenging circumstances force them into a posture of dependency.

3. **Read John 1:14. What do you think it means that Jesus is "the Word"? What does it tell us about Jesus' connection to God?**

4. **During the message, Andy said, "Jesus didn't claim to *have* the best explanation of God. He claimed to *be* the best explanation of God." Respond to that statement. In what ways do you find it challenging, disturbing, or offensive?**

   These two questions are designed to allow group members to wrestle with one of the most offensive aspects of Christianity. It's important that the group environment is safe enough that group members who don't agree with Jesus' claim feel free to say so.

5. **Talk about some of the wrong places you've looked to find out what God is like—religious traditions, your circumstances, nature, within yourself. What limitations did you discover in these attempts to find God?**

6. **At the end of the message, Andy challenged you to read the four Gospels with this question in mind: What do we learn about the Father from the Son? Which gospel will you begin with? What can this group do to help you follow through on this homework?**

   The last two questions are intended to help group members personalize and apply the content. Identifying their own tendencies to look for God in the wrong places sets them up for a richer experience when they read a gospel and ask themselves the question, "What do we learn about the Father from the Son?"

Session 2: Notes for Leading

Big Idea

Jesus came to teach us things we could not learn from nature, space, looking within, or looking around.

To Prepare to Lead the Second Session

- Read John 9:1–34.
- Pray that you and your group members are able to speak transparently about personal pain and suffering. Pray that your group members have the courage to open up about their doubts and fears, and that God meets their openness with mercy and grace.

Discussion Starter

This discussion starter is designed to help you and your group members think about the way you view rules and how that has shaped your interactions with the world and with God.

Discussion Questions

1. **Last week, Andy asked you to read one of the Gospels with this question in mind: *"What do I learn about the Father from the Son?"* What is one insight you gained about God as you read?**

   As you and your group discuss this question, you'll have the opportunity to discuss any personal insights you had while reading during the week. If a group member didn't read, be sure not to make him or her feel guilty.

2. **Have you ever seen someone demonstrate great faith despite great suffering? How did that affect your faith in God?**

3. **Do you ever wonder if your suffering is your fault? If so, how has that shaped your view of God?**

4. **During the message, Andy said, "*God sometimes chooses to display his power through our pain.*" Respond to that statement. How does it bother you? In what ways is it comforting?**

   The next three questions are designed to help you and your group explore and discuss the topics of our pain and God's grace and mercy. This is a complex and emotional topic, so the questions are organized to move from a discussion of other people's pain, to personal experience, and then to how our experiences influence how we view God's role in our pain.

5. **During the message, Andy used an example of the Pharisees allowing their theology to become an obstacle to mercy for a man cured of blindness. In what ways have you seen theology—your own or someone else's—act as an obstacle to mercy?**

   This question offers you and your group the chance to dig into conflicts between theology and mercy in a modern (and even personal) context. The more transparent you are, the richer your discussion will be.

6. **Do you find it difficult to believe that God takes an interest in you individually? Why or why not? What is one thing you can do this week to remind yourself that God *is* interested in you individually?**

   Sometimes there is a divide between what we know in our minds to be true and what we feel in our hearts. This question provides an opportunity for you and your group members to wrestle with an emotional topic that many Christians brush aside with the "right" theological answer. If you or one of your group members is struggling in this area, the group can offer encouragement and accountability.

Session 3: Notes for Leading

Big Idea

Jesus came to elevate the dignity of the individual.

To Prepare to Lead the Third Session

- Read Luke 7:39–40 and Romans 5:7–8.
- Pray that you and your group members have open hearts regarding this challenging topic. Ask God to help you share freely and to change the way you view and treat the people around you.

Discussion Starter

This week's discussion question is designed to help you and your group members reconnect with a time when you may have been treated poorly or treated others poorly depending on the group you were in. The question's purpose is to create an emotional bridge to the material you'll discuss later.

Discussion Questions

1. **In what ways do adults label people? How does this impulse to attach labels to other human beings shape our culture?**

2. **What labels, good or bad, do you carry? How do they shape how you see yourself?**

   The first two questions are intended to help you think about how people are labeled in our culture, as well as how people are treated based on the label they're given.

3. **During the message, Andy said, *"The Christian community should be the most nondiscriminatory, it-doesn't-matter-to-us-who-you-are group of people on the planet."* What are some of the obstacles to the church living up to that calling? What is the cost of not living up to that calling?**

   This question is meant to spur you and your group members into exploring and discussing how successfully the church carries out the mission Jesus gave it. The purpose isn't to create a feeling of guilt or anger. It's to encourage group members to see the church from an outsider's perspective.

4. **Read Romans 5:7–8. How does this passage change the way you view your value as a human being? How does it challenge the way you view others?**

5. **What person or group of people do you power up around, look down on, treat as less than, or maintain a bad attitude toward? What causes you to respond to that person or group the way you do?**

6. **What is one thing you can do this week to begin to treat that person or group with dignity? How can this group support you?**

   The last three questions are intended to help you think about God's view of people and your view of people. The final question then challenges you to think of ways that you can begin to treat with more dignity people with whom it is challenging to interact.

Session 4: Notes for Leading

Big Idea

Jesus came to put religion in its place.

To Prepare to Lead the Fourth Session

- Read Mark 2:24, 27; Isaiah 1:11, 13, 15, 17; and Matthew 22:37–40.
- Pray that your group ends this study well. Ask God to help your group members use the discussions you've had to grow closer to him.

Discussion Starter

This week's discussion starter is designed to help you and your group members think about your own perceptions of and responses to rules. It ties into the main topic but allows you to kick off the discussion in a fun and nonthreatening manner.

Discussion Questions

1. **What are some reasons people find rules comfortable and comforting?**

2. **Are there things about religion that you find constraining or stifling? If so, what are those things?**
   The first two questions are designed to continue and deepen the conversation begun in the Discussion Starter. They give you and your group members the opportunity to think and talk more about the benefits and drawbacks of rules and religion.

3. **Read Isaiah 1:13, 17. How do these verses challenge most people's views of God? What do they tell us about what he values?**
   This question is a springboard from two verses that express God's passion and love for individual people. It's intended to get you thinking through your assumptions about God's values and priorities.

4. **During the message, Andy said, *"Jesus consistently prioritized people over his own religion, customs, and traditions."* Respond to that statement. In what ways does it challenge your assumptions about Jesus?**

5. **Is it difficult for you to believe that God values you above his own rules? Why or why not?**
   Questions 4 and 5 continue the theme that began in question 3. Now, you'll think about how Jesus navigated tensions between religion and compassion as well as connecting those thoughts to your relationship with God.

6. **What is one thing you can do this week to prioritize loving God and loving other people over your religion, customs, and traditions? What can this group do to support you?**
   The final question turns outward, challenging you and your group members to treat others with a love and compassion that reflects the love and compassion God has shown you.

End the session in prayer. Ask your group members if anything came up during the course of the study about which they would like the group to provide continued encouragement and accountability.

Follow DVD Study

No Experience Necessary

Andy Stanley

Lots of people think Christianity is all about doing what Jesus says. But what if doing what Jesus says isn't what Jesus says to do at all? Jesus' invitation is an invitation to relationship, and it begins with a simple request: follow me.

Religion says "Change and you can join us." Jesus says, "Join us and you will change." There's a huge difference. Jesus doesn't expect people to be perfect. He just wants them to follow him. Being a sinner doesn't disqualify anyone. Being an unbeliever doesn't disqualify anyone. In fact, following almost always begins with a sinner and unbeliever taking one small step.

In this eight-session video-based Bible study (participant's guide sold separately), Andy Stanley takes small groups on a journey through the Gospels as he traces Jesus' teaching on what it means to follow.

Sessions include:

1. Jesus Says
2. Next Steps
3. Fearless
4. Follow Wear
5. The Fine Print
6. What I Want to Want
7. Leading Great
8. Unfollow

Available in stores and online!

How to Be Rich: A DVD Study

It's Not What You Have. It's What You Do With What You Have.

Andy Stanley

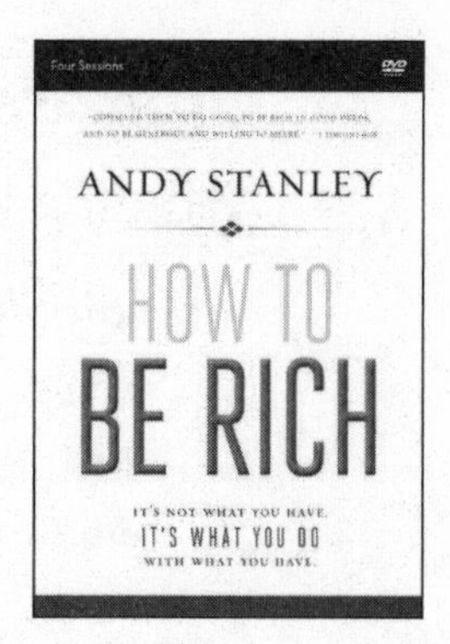

Ever stood in front of a closet full of clothes trying to find something to wear?
Ever traded in a perfectly good car for another...car?
Ever killed some time talking on your cell phone while standing in line to get a newer version of the same phone?

According to author and pastor Andy Stanley, if you answered "yes" to any of those questions, you might be rich.

But you might think, rich is the other guy. Rich is that other family. Rich is having more than you currently have. If that's the case, you can be rich and not know it. You can be rich and not feel it. You can be rich and not act like it. And that is a problem.

In this four-session small group study, Andy Stanley encourages us to consider that we may be richer than we think, and challenges us to consider that we may not be very good at it.

It's one thing to Be Rich.

Andy wants to help us all be GOOD at it!

Sessions include:

1. Congratulations
2. Side Effects
3. Dollar Cost Living
4. Diversify

Staying in Love DVD Study

Falling in Love Is Easy, Staying in Love Requires a Plan

Andy Stanley

We all know what's required to fall in love... a pulse. Falling in love is easy. But staying there—that's something else entirely. With more than a thousand matchmaking services available today and new ones springing up all the time, finding a romantic match can be easier than ever. But staying together with the one you've found seems to be the real challenge.

So, is it possible for two people to fall in love and actually stay there? Absolutely! Let pastor and author Andy Stanley show you how in this four-session, video-based study that also features a separate participant's guide.

Session titles include:

1. The Juno Dilemma
2. Re-Modeling
3. Feelin' It
4. Multiple Choice Marriage

Available in stores and online!